Popular Cat Library

Ragdoll Cat

Gary A. Strobel and Susan A. Nelson

Published in association with T.F.H. Publications, Inc.,
the world's largest and most respected publisher of pet literature

Chelsea House Publishers
Philadelphia

CONTENTS

Popular Cat Library

Abyssinian Cat
American Shorthair Cat
Bengal Cat
Birman Cat
Burmese Cat
Exotic Shorthair Cat
Himalayan Cat
Maine Coon Cat
Persian Cat
Ragdoll Cat
Scottish Fold Cat
Siamese Cat

Publisher's Note: All of the photographs in this book have been coated with FOTO-GLAZE® finish, a special lamination that imparts a new dimension of colorful gloss to the photographs.

Reinforced Library Binding & Super-Highest Quality Boards

This edition © TFH Publications, Inc., 1 TFH Plaza, Neptune City, NJ 07753. This special library bound edition is made expressly for Chelsea House Publishers, a division of Main Line Book Company.

Library of Congress Cataloging-in-Publication Data

Strobel, Gary A.
Guide to owning a ragdoll cat / by Gary A. Strobel and Susan A. Nelson.
p.   cm. — (Popular cat library)
Previously published: Neptune City, N.J. : T.F.H. Publications, 1997.
Summary: A guide to the history, feeding, grooming, exhibition, temperament, health, and breeding of ragdoll cats.
ISBN 0-7910-5466-7 (hc)
1. Ragdoll cat Juvenile literature.   [1. Ragdoll cat. 2. Cats. 3. Pets.]   I. Title.
II. Series.
SF449.R34S77 1999
636.8'3—dc21
                                                                        99-26497
                                                                        CIP

INTRODUCTION

Never before in the history of the cat fancy has a breed taken over the hearts and homes of so many people so quickly. Word of this new and fascinating breed is sweeping the world, and Ragdoll breeders are having trouble keeping up with the demand. The Ragdoll is the gentle giant of the domestic feline world, and, as you will see, the perfect cat for the 21st century.

This book is written for new or potential Ragdoll owners, those who already own and love their Ragdolls, and those simply interested in learning more about this incredible breed. We have also attempted to make this book breeder friendly, as the ultimate authority on your Ragdoll is its breeder.

Blue mitted male Ragdoll kitten. Photo by Muncy Smith.

The Ragdoll cat of today was developed from the unlikely combination of three feral cats in Riverside, California. Lots of stories have been told about the origins and characteristics of Ragdolls, but one common thread runs through them all: the purebred Ragdoll cat owes its existence to a woman named Ann Baker and a female cat named Josephine.

Josephine was a feral cat living in a cat colony on the property of Ann Baker's neighbor. She had become somewhat tame while being nursed back to health following an automobile accident. It was Ann Baker who recognized special qualities in Josephine's subsequent litters and obtained a female kitten from one of Josephine's litters, naming it Buckwheat. Buckwheat was a black self female, meaning that she was solid black. Ann Baker's neighbor also kept one of Josephine's kittens, a pointed male with white mittens named Daddy Warbucks. Ann Baker obtained a daughter of Daddy Warbucks and Josephine, Fugianna, who was the first bicolor Ragdoll. Using the stud services of her neighbor's cat, Daddy Warbucks, Ann Baker used these cats to establish the Ragdoll breed.

Ragdolls have become the fastest growing and most lovable breed of cat ever developed. Owners readily admit that they are captivated by their Ragdolls' sweet temperament, beautiful coat, generous size, and big blue eyes. Each of the following chapters will introduce you to one important aspect of Ragdoll ownership, from understanding special Ragdoll traits to selecting your Ragdoll, from making your home "Ragdoll friendly" to caring for your Ragdoll's health, and from breeding to showing your Ragdoll. As Ragdolls can live to be twenty years old, you will have many years to discover for yourself exactly why Ragdolls are held to be such a special breed by those who know and love them.

WHAT'S SO SPECIAL ABOUT RAGDOLLS?

THE RAGDOLL PERSONALITY IS PURRFECT

A more loving cat you'll never find. Ragdolls are strictly indoor cats that love and depend upon their owners. In exchange, owners receive an endless supply of love and affection from their Ragdolls. Many Ragdoll owners have compared their Ragdoll's personality to that of a loyal canine. Ragdolls are eager to interact, and there are numerous accounts of Ragdolls fetching their favorite toy, learning how to shake hands, and sitting up on command.

The Ragdoll personality is characteristically warm and friendly. Your Ragdoll will want to be with you all the time. You'll be met at the door when you arrive home and followed around the house, even into the bathroom. When taking a shower, expect your Ragdoll to watch and wait patiently for you right outside the shower. As you push aside the curtain or shower door, you'll see your Ragdoll looking up at you with those big blue eyes. Your Ragdoll will be curious and eager to meet and greet guests to your home.

If you want a lap cat, the Ragdoll is for you. Ragdolls need their owner's attention and lots of love. If not on your lap, your Ragdoll will be lying nearby. Very few breeds of cat offer the

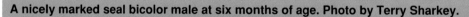

A nicely marked seal bicolor male at six months of age. Photo by Terry Sharkey.

intimate companionship characteristic of the Ragdoll. Persians are purchased for their beautiful coats. Maine Coons are purchased for their large size. Siamese are purchased for their blue eyes. Himalayans are purchased for their dramatic color points. Ragdolls are purchased for their purrfect personality. As a bonus, you get a beautiful coat, large, stunning blue eyes, calm laid-back personality, and the classic pointed pattern—all together in one fabulous package called the Ragdoll.

THE RAGDOLL VOICE IS QUIET

Ragdolls go about their daily activities with little vocalization. They don't meow insistently like some other breeds, but Ragdolls can be trained to respond to your voice. When Ragdolls do vocalize, their voice always reflects the way they are feeling.

Each separate Ragdoll vocalization expresses a different emotion. If your Ragdoll is feeling happy, you're likely to hear a short, upbeat meow. Turn toward the "meow," and your Ragdoll will be looking at you intently. Your Ragdoll just wants a little attention. When your Ragdoll is feeling lonely, you will hear a longer, more plaintive meow. You can be certain that you are expected to stop what you are doing, pick up your Ragdoll, and administer a good snuggle. If your Ragdoll takes a nap and awakens to find that you have left the room, it will pace the house crying for you. At times like this,

A seal mitted Ragdoll named Dolly with a young member of her human family. Well mannered children go nicely with gentle Ragdolls. Photo by Susan Nelson.

it is best to call out to your Ragdoll so that it can find you. Your Ragdoll will run to you, craving companionship. When your Ragdoll is feeling sleepy and wants to curl up in your arms, you could be blessed with a purr that ends in a trill or a chirp. If it's your bedtime, too, your Ragdoll will curl up purring on your chest or snuggle up beside you. What a lovely way to go to sleep. In the morning, your Ragdoll will chirp happily to you when it realizes that you are awake.

THE RAGDOLL LIVES ONLY INDOORS

Ragdolls belong indoors.

Whether you have a studio apartment or a mansion, your Ragdoll will be at home indoors with you. Ragdolls are reputed to be so docile that they will not defend themselves from other cats and animals. They are so beautiful and friendly that they are susceptible to being "catnapped." Outside cats can spread diseases to your Ragdoll. Keep your Ragdoll indoors to protect it from harm.

THE RAGDOLL IS EASY TO TRAIN

When you get your Ragdoll kitten at eight to sixteen weeks old, it should already be litter box trained. Often, Ragdoll breeders report that kittens are using the litter box by four to five weeks of age. This attests to their ability to learn quickly by imitating their mother's behavior.

Your kitten should be trained to a scratching post by the time you bring it home. Cats scratch and manicure their claws when they are feeling good. So, you don't want to jump up and yell "No" if

Desilu, a blue colorpoint. The large blue eyes are a hallmark of the breed. Photo by Susan Nelson.

your Ragdoll forgets to use the scratching post. You'll only succeed in upsetting it and making it run away from you. Instead, if you find your Ragdoll scratching a forbidden spot, just walk over calmly and pick it up in a matter-of-fact manner while saying "No," bring it to the nearest scratching post, and begin demonstrating what you want by scratching the area yourself. Your Ragdoll will very often begin to imitate you. To help with this training, provide more than one permissible scratching area. Be especially careful to have a scratching area close to where your kitten sleeps, as it will want to scratch upon awakening. With Ragdolls, this training is fairly easy to accomplish.

Ragdolls have a playful nature. Many Ragdoll owners have reported that their Ragdolls are actually able to learn to fetch. If your Ragdoll has a favorite toy such as a knotted shoe lace or any easy-to-carry object, your Ragdoll may retrieve it when it is thrown across the room. Sometimes, your Ragdoll may come up to you with a toy as if it is begging you to play fetch. Take advantage of this natural behavior and toss the toy. See what happens. If your Ragdoll brings it back, toss it again.

When your kitten is small, you need to teach it patience. Ragdolls are docile by nature, but, like any cat, they need to learn patience. When you are holding your kitten, it is important that you—not it— make the decision as to when it gets let down. If a Ragdoll is

Will the "real" Ragdoll please stand up? This seal mitted male seems surprised to be caught by the photographer! Photo by Eva Davis.

allowed to get down anytime it wants to, it begins to think that it is in charge and will become difficult to handle when it reaches, say, fifteen pounds. In order to avoid being used as a launching pad, this is also the time to teach it to expect to be placed solidly on the ground rather than letting it leap from your arms. So, if your Ragdoll struggles to get down, firmly and lovingly maintain your hold until *you* decide that it's time to place it on the ground. Talk gently to your kitten during this time. Patience must be taught at the earliest possible age, preferably

two to four months old. Once your Ragdoll is past this age, the training is more difficult, and it will take rewards, such as a special treat, to encourage patience.

THE RAGDOLL IS A SPECIAL COMPANION

From their laid-back personalities and quiet voices to their playful nature and craving of attention, Ragdolls are special, loving companions. Whether you adopt one, two, or half a dozen, your life will be filled with a special warmth because of their presence.

SELECTING YOUR RAGDOLL

RAGDOLL COLORS AND PATTERNS

The standard Ragdoll comes in four colors and three patterns; and all Ragdolls have blue eyes and a soft, non-matting hair coat. Kittens' coats may not be as soft as adults' coats, as kittens go through a four- to six-month growth cycle that usually alters the hair coat's texture. Each Ragdoll color and pattern is discussed below. Some breeders are presently working to add new and unusual colors to the breed standard, and these are discussed later in this chapter.

STANDARD COLORS

All Ragdolls are pointed cats. This means that they have color on their ears, faces, legs, and tails, with a much lighter, contrasting body color. Ragdolls come in four standard colors: seal, chocolate, blue, and frost (sometimes called lilac).

Seal Ragdolls have points that are a deep seal brown. Their bodies should have fawn to cream color shading, although some may have darker shading. Their nose

Note the nice ruff, which is the collarlike projection of fur around the neck, on this seal mitted male. Photo by Gary Strobel.

and paw pad leather should be a deep seal brown.

Chocolate Ragdolls have points that are a light milk chocolate color. Their bodies should have ivory to cream shading. Their nose and paw pad leather should be what some have called a "burnt rose" tone. However, the chocolate Ragdoll is not yet standardized, and there is still discussion among breeders as to what comprises a true chocolate. Some chocolates have darker nose leather, and this is permissible.

Blue Ragdolls have points that are slate blue to silver, with a generally gray appearance. Their bodies can be ivory to bluish white. The nose and paw pad leather should be slate blue.

Frost Ragdolls have points that are lilac to pinkish beige. Their bodies should be milk white, and the nose and paw pad leather should be pink to lavender.

STANDARD PATTERNS

The three standard Ragdoll

patterns are colorpoint, mitted, and bicolor.

Colorpoint Ragdolls have darker color on their ears, face, legs, feet, and tail. Their body color is lighter than their point color. The chest and chin are usually lighter in color but are closer to the body color.

Mitted Ragdolls are identical to colorpoint Ragdolls, except that they have white paws, chin, and chest. Their front paws have little white mittens. On their back legs, the mittens extend halfway up their legs, becoming white boots. Their bodies, with the exception of their white chin and chest, are at least a shade lighter than their point color.

Bicolor Ragdolls have darker color on their ears, face, and tail. However, a bicolor's face is characterized by a white, inverted "V." The stomach, all four legs, the feet, and ruff are white. The body color should be at least a shade lighter than the point color, and the bicolor Ragdoll may have various markings of white and color patches across the back. This distinctive appearance sets the Ragdoll apart from all other breeds. The bicolor's nose and paw pad color is pink.

NEW AND UNUSUAL COLORS

In the spring of 1997, the Ragdoll Fancier's Club International voted to accept the lynx pattern and the red color. The lynx pattern does not affect the four colors or the three basic patterns of the Ragdoll. It merely adds a striking striped effect to the face, legs, and tail, in addition

A Ragdoll's weight can range from 12 to 20 pounds. This blue colorpoint male is a very large example of the breed. Photo by Susan Nelson.

to contrasting white on the inside of the ears. This pattern was present in Ann Baker's early breedings, but she sold these kittens to other breeders, who began to reintroduce it just a few years ago.

Colors to look for due to the acceptance of the red are the tortie point and flame point. Ragdolls with this red gene are presently in development. Tortie points have a tricolor, somewhat mottled appearance to their point markings, while the flame points have a reddish hue to their points.

It is the authors' opinion that whatever new colors are developed, the Ragdoll should remain a large, pointed cat with blue eyes and a non-matting hair coat. And the Ragdoll personality should never be compromised. As is the case with all of the major breeds, these new colors will probably eventually be accepted and standards set by the majority vote of Ragdoll breeders.

FINDING THE PERFECT RAGDOLL
Go to Local Cat Shows

There are many ways to find your perfect Ragdoll kitten. One good way to get started is to go to local cat shows. Usually, there will be at least one Ragdoll entered. Sometimes, there may be no local cat shows in your area or no Ragdolls entered in your local shows. If this is the case, skip to the next paragraph. However, if you are lucky enough to be able to attend a show where Ragdolls are being exhibited, talk to the people showing the Ragdolls and find out who their breeders are and if they are happy with them. This is a good way to get to see Ragdolls as well as talk with people who actually own them. However, don't expect to be allowed to hold or touch the Ragdolls, as it is not proper etiquette at a cat show to touch, or even ask to touch, other peoples' cats. This is because of the risk of spreading disease from one cat to another.

Read the National Cat Magazines

Another way to find your perfect Ragdoll is to get a copy of one or more of the following magazines: *Cat Fancy, Cats Magazine,* or a yearly publication called *Cats U.S.A.* Look at the breeders' directories located at the back of these publications, and locate the breeders nearest your home. If there are no local breeders, contact the ones nearest to you. Be aware that shipping kittens is not at all unusual. And Ragdolls' temperament enables them to take shipping in stride.

A lilac (frost) bicolor with a beautiful, soft, non-matting coat, as all true Ragdolls have. Photo by Gary Strobel.

Connect with Breeders on the Internet

The Internet is also a good way to find Ragdoll breeders near you. Using the larger search engines, simply type in "Ragdoll Cats." You will find a wealth of information, including breeders located near your home.

Check out Several Catteries

Once you have a list of breeders in mind, make arrangements to visit as many catteries as you can. Although it is often difficult to resist buying the first kitten you see, try to wait until you have had a chance to check out several catteries and meet several breeders. However, many a beautiful kitten has been purchased on the first visit. Sometimes, a kitten may be sold if you delay purchase, as Ragdolls are very popular and usually in short supply. Yet, you can take your time in making a selection, as Ragdoll breeders generally plan litters so that they will have kittens available on an ongoing basis. If you are patient, they will be able to supply you with the Ragdoll of your dreams.

In some areas, breeders may be few and far between, in which case you may want to be prepared to leave a deposit on the color and pattern of your choice. Some patterns and colors may not be readily available, and you will need to place a deposit to reserve your Ragdoll. Remember, you are searching for a companion for the next fifteen years or more. Be selective, and be willing to wait for what you want. You owe this to yourself and your future companion.

A lilac (frost) bicolor being carefully assessed by a judge. Going to shows is one good way of obtaining information about where to select a Ragdoll kitten. Photo by Kathy Lam.

When visiting catteries, there are several things to keep in mind. Plan to visit only one cattery or breeder per day, to prevent diseases or germs being spread from cattery to cattery. When you arrive at a breeder's home, look to see whether cats are roaming freely about the house. If so, this is a good sign. Make sure the premises appear and smell reasonably clean. Remember though, that the breeder cannot control when a cat might choose to visit the litter

A three-week-old litter of Ragdoll kittens eager to start exploring their world. Photo by Susan Nelson.

box. Check whether the cats are outgoing or run away from you when you try to pet them. Observe whether the general appearance of the cats is healthy. Red eyes? Sneezing? Runny nose? Ribs showing? Bloated stomach? Excessive scratching? Dirty ears inside? All of these conditions are signs of possible problems.

Although some breeders may not have you visit the youngest kittens in the "queening room," the room where the kittens are born and spend their first three weeks of life, the breeder should be willing to share with you the rest of the cattery. Don't be afraid to ask to see the mother and father of your prospective kitten and where the breeding males are housed. If the breeder has nothing to hide, there should be no problem with allowing you to walk through the cattery.

While you are visiting catteries, do not forget that the breeder you choose must be someone you feel comfortable talking to, as you may wish or need to contact him or her with specific questions throughout your Ragdoll's lifetime. Breeders appreciate notes and pictures telling them how your Ragdoll is doing and what sorts of behavior and tricks your Ragdoll has learned. When you purchase your kitten, you and your breeder are beginning a relationship spanning fifteen to twenty years.

THE PURCHASE CONTRACT
Each breeder has a purchase contract. The main components of a purchase contract are the health guarantee, the vaccination records, and the agreement to have the kitten spayed or neutered.

Two of the first purebred Ragdoll flamepoints in the world. They were bred from original stock of Ann Baker. Note the almond-shaped eyes and Ragdoll muzzle. Photo by Susan Nelson.

The health guarantee is of primary importance. Most breeders guarantee their kittens to be healthy and free of parasites, such as fleas, ear mites, and round worms, at the time of pick up. In order to protect yourself and ensure your kitten's ongoing good health, most breeders would like to have you visit your veterinarian as soon as possible after the kitten goes home, usually within seventy-two hours. You might want to arrange to stop by your veterinarian on the way home from the breeder's with your kitten. This way, your kitten won't need to be removed from its new environment during the critical first week of settling into its new home.

Reputable breeders will also guarantee their kittens against genetic problems for at least the first year. Some breeders will put restrictions on declawing kittens.

Others will restrict to whom and where the kitten goes in the event that you can no longer take care of it. These are all individual differences between breeders. And most of these requests are reasonable. If you have any questions or concerns about the contract, discuss them with your breeder, as your breeder will give you the rationale for these restrictions.

Some contracts may address the issue of whether to vaccinate your kitten for feline infectious peritonitis (FIP). This vaccine is controversial due to its use of a modified live virus. Some breeders fear that the administration of this vaccine could infect the kitten with FIP. However, most veterinarians believe the contrary. As with all purebred cats, it is best to err on the side of caution, as administering the FIP vaccine could void the health warranty.

Since Ragdolls are strictly indoor cats, their chance of being exposed to this virus is minimal. Follow your breeder's advice, as most veterinarians are not familiar with Ragdolls because they are still relatively rare.

When you pick up your Ragdoll kitten, your breeder will give you a written record of its first vaccinations. Bring this with you to the veterinarian. The most common vaccinations that your kittens should have had are the three-in-one distemper vaccine, with or without *chlamydia*. Each breeder will have his or her own personalized vaccination protocol. In general, however, your kitten will have had its first

Sometimes a small white blaze appears on the nose, such as the one on this seal mitted male Ragdoll. Photo by Marcella Frenken.

distemper shot between the ages of six and eight weeks old, the second between the ages of eight and twelve weeks old, and at least one or two more distemper shots after twelve weeks of age. Yearly boosters must be given.

The feline leukemia vaccine should not be given until at least twelve to sixteen weeks of age. There is also controversy surrounding this vaccination. Ragdolls are indoor cats and their chance of being exposed to this virus is minimal. Therefore, some

breeders question taking the risk, as any vaccine can have side effects. In any case, *all vaccines* given to Ragdolls must be killed virus vaccines. Do not allow your veterinarian to give anything else. Each time you bring your Ragdoll in for shots, remind your veterinarian to give killed vaccines *only*. A good veterinarian will welcome your reminder. If you board or show your Ragdoll or have an indoor-outdoor cat living with your Ragdoll, this greatly increases the chance of harmful viruses entering your home, in which case the risk of vaccine side effects is likely outweighed by the risk of contracting a serious virus.

When purchasing your Ragdoll, you will be asked to neuter or spay any kitten that will not be used for breeding. You will be asked to pay a much higher price for breeding and/or show-quality Ragdolls versus pet-quality Ragdolls. Females that are not spayed run the risk of uterine infections called pyometra after several estrus cycles. Males that are not neutered may spray pungent urine on furniture to mark their territory. Unneutered females may spray urine to attract a mate.

Generally, neutered cats enjoy a longer life and better health. Most breeders request that female Ragdolls be spayed between the ages of four and seven months. Males should be neutered when they are a bit older, usually not before seven months. If your breeder does not have a preference, talk it over with your veterinarian. Most breeders will withhold registration papers until receiving written proof from a veterinarian that your cat has been spayed or neutered. This proof can usually be supplied by furnishing your breeder with a photocopy of the paid invoice from your veterinarian.

Be certain that you read and understand the purchase contract before you purchase your Ragdoll. Some contract terms can be individually negotiated with the breeder. Don't hesitate to ask questions and get answers. A good breeder will not be reluctant to discuss any contract term with you.

The "hour glass" blaze on this six-week-old seal mitted male is very distinct. Photo by Muncy Smith.

YOUR RAGDOLL'S PAPERS

When the kitten that you select was born, the breeder filed a litter registration form with the appropriate cat association. When you take your kitten home, either you will be given a form to fill out and send to the same cat association, along with the registration fee, or you will be told that the registration form will be given to you upon proof of neutering or spaying. The form will have a place on it where the breeder can restrict breeding and showing. Some breeders will not restrict showing pet-quality Ragdolls in the alter class, and you should ask your breeder's policy before you buy. If you do not plan to show your Ragdoll, you are not required to register it. However, the fee is minimal; and if you should ever want to show your kitten, registration is required. So, you might as well obtain your Ragdoll's final registration papers at the earliest opportunity.

ONE RAGDOLL OR TWO?

Ragdolls easily adjust to multi-cat households. You may select one kitten and decide later to add a playmate. Or you may select two kittens at once. If you decide on a solo kitten, it will quickly adjust to your schedule. There is also a chance that a solo kitten will

Owning two Ragdolls is twice as fun as owning just one. Additionally , they can keep each other company when you are not at home. Photo by Elsa Brent.

bond with you more strongly. If you later add a new kitten, they will probably have an adjustment period of about one to two weeks. During this time, they may hiss a bit at each other to establish dominance. This is normal feline behavior; however, you should carefully monitor your kittens during this time to be certain that they are adjusting well. If they hiss more than you would like, give them a break from each other for a few hours daily by letting them play in different rooms. You will be rewarded for your patience when you see them playing happily together.

Most breeders suggest that you purchase two kittens at the same time. That way, your Ragdoll will have a companion even when you must be away at work, running errands, or on vacation. Unless you are at home nearly twenty-four hours a day, there is a chance that a solo kitten, after being taken from its litter mates, could be lonely and stressed. Two kittens are double the fun and double the love, and you will have double the enjoyment watching them roll and tumble, groom each other, and sleep nestled together. The choice is yours.

Unlike other kittens, two Ragdolls will generally play quietly together. They will not climb draperies or tear up your home; thus, they are great for even small apartments. Either way, after selecting one kitten or two, you won't want to miss the experience of having a Ragdoll in your life.

HOW TO MAKE YOUR HOME RAGDOLL-FRIENDLY

ELIMINATE HAZARDS IN YOUR HOME

Before bringing your Ragdoll home, examine your home from the perspective of a tiny kitten. Getting down on your hands and knees may seem silly, but it will help you to realize what may present a hazard to your Ragdoll. Remember, your little Ragdoll is full of curiosity and anxious to explore its world. He or she will find any crack or crevice and climb in. There will not be a square inch of your home that is not left unexplored. Therefore, it is your responsibility to assure that your new kitten's home is safe.

Hazards include electrical cords, open toilet seats, unattended flames on stoves and candles, hot liquid in potpourri bowls, hot stove burners, wall or space heaters, fans, open oven doors, open refrigerator doors, open dishwasher doors, open trash compactors, open clothes dryers, unattended dishwater and bath water, all cleaning supplies, tiny objects that could be swallowed, open fireplaces, open

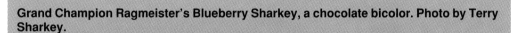

Grand Champion Ragmeister's Blueberry Sharkey, a chocolate bicolor. Photo by Terry Sharkey.

windows, loose window screens, balconies, electric paper shredders set on automatic, thread, string, rubber bands, ribbon, yarn, and sharp objects such as broken glass, discarded staples, needles, pins, feathers bitten from kitty toys, and knives. Beware of store-bought cat toys with small parts that can tug off and be swallowed. Be careful when closing open drawers, as kittens love to crawl inside and behind them to explore. If you have any doors on rollers, be especially careful to check that your kitten is not behind them when you close them, as toes, paws, or tails can be crushed or worse. Be especially careful with

A beautiful blue lynx colorpoint male showing off his huge tail. Photo by Barbara McKenzie-Wardell.

what you use to decorate for any holidays that you observe, as broken glass ornaments and small parts that can be chewed off could be deadly to your Ragdoll.

The injuries resulting from the above hazards can be heart wrenching. Kittens can get severe electrical shocks and/or burns and die from biting into electrical cords that are not covered with foam insulation tubes. These tubes, which are available at most hardware stores, have slits along the length of the tube. The slits allow easy insertion of several electrical cords into one tube. Drowning can occur when a kitten falls into an open toilet, bath, or sink of dishwater. Flames, space heaters, hot liquid, open oven doors, and hot stove burners can catch fur on fire, burn right through the skin, or cause severe blistering of tender paw pads. Open appliance doors can cause suffocation if closed without checking for kitty. Kittens have been killed when clothes were quickly thrown into a clothes dryer and the drying cycle started. Paws can be caught and cut in electric fans and paper shredders. Since cats have little spines on their tongues that force them to swallow whatever they get even partially inside their mouths, they can swallow staples, pins, thread, and myriad other objects. Once inside the digestive tract, these objects can pierce the intestine or twist up inside the bowel, causing an obstruction. Household cleaners can be licked up or transferred to the kitten's mouth by self-grooming after the kitten walks across a surface cleaned with a poisonous substance.

A lilac (frost) bicolor female posing for a cameo. In bicolors, the chest, stomach, legs, feet, and ruff are white. Photo by Susan Nelson.

Check all labels; if you see that any label has a poison control telephone number listed, don't buy it. Finally, many cats have been maimed or died falling through open windows and loose window screens; many more have died because their owners never realized that they would jump from an open balcony. An additional hazard is living plants. Before exposing your Ragdoll to any indoor or outdoor plants that you may already have in your home, consult a good gardening book to determine whether they are poisonous. If in doubt, bring them to your local nursery for identification. Never purchase cut flowers that are poisonous, as cats will sample vases of flowers. If you do have any poisonous plants, replace them with silk plants. Nothing is more heartbreaking than watching a pet suffer from an accidental poisoning that could have been prevented.

Although our list of hazards may seem quite lengthy, you must protect against all of them. If you do, you will save your kitten potential injury and yourself trauma and unexpected veterinary bills.

IT'S EASY TO ACCIDENTALLY STEP ON A KITTEN

Your new Ragdoll will tend to want to be with you all the time and is very easily stepped on. You will be amazed at how quickly a kitten or grown cat can silently move from one area of a room to a

A blue bicolor male. Note the well-defined color of the ears, mask, and tail. Photo by Pauline Somers.

point right under your feet without your realizing it. Crushing a Ragdoll's leg, or worse, is not something you want to experience. Therefore, always be cautious walking when there is a kitten in the house. They can dart underfoot from behind sofas and tables when you least expect to see them. They also can dart underfoot in an attempt to race you to the top or bottom of the stairs. Be especially cautious when sitting at your computer or desk, as your Ragdoll will have a tendency to lie under the chair, either beside the leg or against the wheel caster, in an effort to be close to you. If your Ragdoll sleeps with you and you need to get out of bed in the dark, it is best to shuffle your feet as you walk. An ounce of prevention can save a huge veterinary bill.

RAGDOLL-FRIENDLY TOYS

Ragdolls need toys. They need a wide variety of toys that can be rotated on a weekly basis, or else they will become quickly bored by them. However, Ragdolls are not "picky." They will play with anything from an empty cardboard tissue tube or empty thread spool to a wad of paper or expensive store-bought toys. Many an expensive toy has been purchased only to lie dormant as a kitten chooses the crumpled-up piece of paper instead. But toys are a necessity if you want to keep your Ragdoll from making up its own games using your things.

The main thing to consider when selecting toys for your Ragdoll is whether parts can break off and be swallowed or whether the toy itself is so small that it could possibly be swallowed or lodged in the mouth or throat. Never let your Ragdoll have unsupervised access to toys with feathers, string, yarn, or ribbon. If the toys that you purchase come with bells, either cut them off or stitch them down securely. Better yet, save these toys for interactive play. Also, it is best to cut the tail off those cute, little furry toy mice. The tail can be bitten off and swallowed. Care in toy selection will eliminate potential hazards.

Since your Ragdoll most enjoys your company, be certain to have several interactive toys in reserve. These are toys on a string or piece of elastic or toys suspended from a wand or "fishing pole." To avoid frustrating your Ragdoll, let it "catch" the "prey" about every third time you entice it to pounce. Start out slowly, quicken the pace, and taper it down again before putting away the interactive toys. This will let your kitten or adult Ragdoll burn off any excess energy and become even more relaxed than usual before it's time for bed. Since all felines are nocturnal, you will need to help your Ragdoll adjust to your schedule, and a nightly play time will do the trick. Your Ragdoll is an indoor cat and depends upon you for stimulation and exercise. Be certain to keep the interactive toys in a closed closet when not in use, as interactive toys tend to have feathers, string, and bells attached to them.

Kittens love boxes, any boxes. Try cutting out holes in a couple of places and putting a terry cloth towel inside the box and/or a safe toy or ball. Your Ragdoll will enjoy jumping through the holes, playing with the toy, and relaxing inside the box. A shallow box can be made into an inexpensive "kitty tease" by putting a couple of jingle balls inside, taping the box securely closed, and cutting out small circles and squares for your Ragdoll to reach through to bat at the balls.

Paper bags from the grocery store or mall also can provide hours of fun for your kitten or adult Ragdoll. Be certain to cut through any handles so that your Ragdoll doesn't accidentally slip its head through the handle and get caught. As with human children, kittens should never be allowed to play with plastic bags.

One of the all-time favorite toys that your kitten

Seal mitted male patiently awaiting the return of his owner. Ragdoll cats will often meet you at the door. Photo by Susan Nelson.

will love is a large, donut-like toy with an accessible ball that your kitten can bat and watch as it rolls around inside the track. It will also enjoy playing the game with you.

Kitty condos and cat towers are wonderful playthings that can double as sleeping quarters. They come fully carpeted or partially covered with sisal rope. Unlike carpet, sisal rope is easily replaced if it begins to look shabby from nail grooming. Towers using only carpet tend to be torn to shreds as time goes by.

Offer your kitten a wide variety

of toys to choose from, and let it decide its favorites.

HOUSEHOLD PLAY AREAS

Some Ragdoll owners set aside a room in their home as a designated playroom. It can be your bedroom. This room is used when the owner is away. It usually contains a litter box in one corner, dry food and water as far away from the litter box as

Scratching posts are essential in any household with a cat. The one shown here features both carpeting and sisal. Photo by Carla Applegate.

possible, a wide assortment of toys, a scratching post, and a cat bed. When your kitten is young, it is important to have such a semi-confined area to leave it in when you are away so that it can't get lost or wedged somewhere in your home and separated from its litter box.

SHOPPING LIST FOR YOUR FUTURE RAGDOLL

Obtain the following items for your kitten before bringing it home, and both of you will be happier for it.

Cat Carrier

Think safety first, and buy a sturdy carrier for your Ragdoll. Don't get one to fit your kitten, get one to fit a twelve-to-twenty pound cat. This means a carrier of medium size, as you will want to use it in the future to take your cat to the vet or shows or out for a drive or on vacation. A carrier will prevent your kitten from getting

under the gas or brake pedal while you are bringing it home from the breeder. It is will also protect your kitten from injury when traveling with you. Put a nice, warm blanket or towel on the bottom of the carrier to make your kitten's trip home cozy. Either wedge the carrier between the seats or wrap the seat belt around it and lock the seat belt into place. If the seat belt will not stretch around your carrier, tie the seat belt to the handle on top of the carrier. In the unlikely event of an accident, an unsecured carrier could be ejected from your car.

You need not keep a litter box in the carrier with your Ragdoll, but on trips of more than two hours, you may want to stop and offer it an opportunity to use the litter box. We have found that keeping a litter box on the floor of the back seat is a big help when traveling with our Ragdolls. We stop the car, get into the back seat with our Ragdoll, close the car doors, and open the carrier door. Our Ragdoll comes out for a stretch, and we simply place it in the litter box. We give it a chance to relax for about five minutes and offer a little food and water. If it doesn't need to use the litter box after five minutes, we place it back into the carrier and offer it another opportunity an hour or two later. We never drive with a cat loose in the car.

When not in use, we leave the carrier sitting in the house with

and litter scoop. Start with a small, low-sided litter box that your kitten can climb into easily. You may choose either pressed paper, regular clay or clay clumping litter, or one of the many wheat or corn pellet-formed litters that are now available. Generally, kittens prefer the finer, sand-type litter as opposed to chunky litter. Ask your breeder what type of litter the kitten is used to, as this will make the transition to your home easier and

A lilac (frost) bicolor female named Misty. The Ragdoll mask appears in the shape of an inverted "V" and extends to the outer edge of the eyes. Photo by Susan Nelson.

the door open in a cozy spot and place a soft terry towel inside. That way, our Ragdolls get used to napping and relaxing inside their carriers. So, we never have a problem putting our Ragdolls into their carriers for trips to the veterinarian or cat shows. If you bring out the carrier only when it is time to go to the vet, you will find your Ragdoll putting on a quick disappearing act as soon as it sees you with its carrier.

Litter Box, Litter, and Litter Scoop

The next most important purchases are the litter box, litter,

prevent most accidents. If you decide to change litters, gradually add it to the litter box until the old litter is completely displaced. As your kitten grows, you may want to increase the size of the litter box. If your kitten desires privacy or tends to scratch litter over the sides of its box, get a covered litter box. We have found a sturdy metal scoop to be most serviceable. A small bathroom mat in front of the litter box helps lessen litter tracking. Pet stores also carry a rubber mat designed for this purpose. Whatever litter box and litter you choose, proper

Your Ragdoll will appreciate a nice, soft cat bed. Be sure to purchase one that will comfortably accommodate your kitten when it is fully grown. Photo by Susan Nelson.

litter box maintenance is a basic requirement for a healthy, happy Ragdoll.

We have a hint for optimal litter box maintenance that you may choose to try to prevent any litter box odor problem from developing. It takes a bit more time, but it is well worth the effort. Once you find a litter pan and litter that your Ragdoll likes and readily uses, keep the litter box and litter clean by following these suggestions. At least once each month, depending upon the type of litter that you use and the number of cats that you own, empty and throw away all litter. Scrape the bottom and sides of the box clean. Take the box outside and rinse the bottom pan with pressurized water from the garden hose. Place about a cup of regular bleach into the pan and carefully swirl it around to wet the bottom and sides of the pan. Let it sit for about five minutes. Then, fill it halfway with water and rinse once or twice. Dry the box with paper toweling and let it sit in the sun for about 10 minutes. Spray the bottom and sides of the box with a non-stick cooking spray. Let the box sit for about five minutes and wipe down any wet areas. Next, put at least three inches of litter in the pan. The bleach helps cut down on lingering odors, and the cooking spray helps used litter clumps to pop easily from the bottom and/or sides of the box. Twice daily, sift

Blue mitted male relaxing in his cat tunnel. Ragdolls love to rest in warm, cozy places. Photo by Susanne Nielsen.

and remove soiled litter using the litter scoop. Add litter as necessary to keep the level at three inches. Try this method and see if it doesn't make a difference.

Bed

In addition to its carrier and any cat tower that you have provided, your Ragdoll needs at least one bed it can call its own. Don't let it choose your favorite chair as its bed. A bed can be as simple as a cardboard box with a towel inside. The day you bring your Ragdoll home, help it adjust by showing it to its bed right after it has been allowed to inspect its litter box. Give it a toy or bite of dry food, pet it, and let it know that the bed belongs to it exclusively. Watch your Ragdoll to see where it prefers to sleep. If it doesn't sleep in its bed but consistently sleeps in one spot, try moving its bed to that spot.

Scratching Post

If you do not have room for a cat tower, you will still need a scratching post to prevent your Ragdoll from grooming its claws on your sofa. Be certain to get a post that will allow a full-grown cat to stretch out completely and pull vigorously without causing the post to tip over. Be assured that Ragdolls are extremely easy to train to a scratching post. We have found that if we just pretend to scratch the post and encourage our Ragdoll to copy us, the task is accomplished in less than a week. Of course, you must consistently demonstrate the preferred behavior. Demonstrating just one time probably won't be enough for even the most intelligent Ragdoll.

Scratching posts offer hours of healthy exercise and enjoyment for cats and kittens while preventing them from damaging furniture. Photo courtesy of Four Paws.

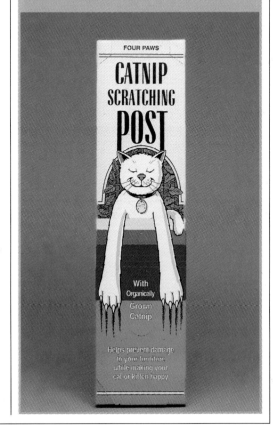

FOUR PAWS

CATNIP SCRATCHING POST

With Organically Grown Catnip

Helps prevent damage to your furniture while making your cat or kitten happy

A lilac (frost) bicolor kitten enjoying a favorite feline pastime—catnapping. Photo by Susan Nelson.

Food and Water Bowls

Your kitten should have its own bowls for food and water. Plastic retains food odors; glass does not. Get three bowls: one for water, one for dry food, and one for wet food. If you have two kittens, they can share for a few weeks, but they should eventually be given their own bowls so that they won't be required to jockey for dominance at the feeding bowl as they grow larger.

Be certain to clean your kitten's water bowl at least daily since food particles will collect in the bottom of it. Since you will be feeding your kitten at least breakfast and dinner, it is easy to remember to change the water twice daily. Your kitten cannot have too much fresh water available. Your kitten's wet food bowl should be washed and *thoroughly* rinsed with hot water when serving each meal. Be mindful that soap residue left on feeding utensils can make any cat ill. Hot water can help to kill bacterial growth on the bowls. Giving each cat its own food and water bowls and keeping them clean prevent disease.

Grooming Supplies

You will want to purchase a flea comb, a metal slicker brush, a high-quality nail clipper, cotton swabs, cotton balls or cotton squares for cleaning nose, ears, and eyes, a toothbrush and toothpaste made especially for kittens, and a gentle shampoo. Your Ragdoll will enjoy the personal interaction of being groomed by you. Begin a grooming routine within the first week and continue it throughout your kitten's life to eliminate parasites, such as fleas, and formation of hairballs in the stomach.

Do not bathe your kitten until it needs it, as the first bath can be very stressful, and you want your kitten's transition to its new home to be as smooth as possible. Occasionally, your kitten may get feces in the hair around its bottom or on its paws. This does not call for a full bath. Simply rinsing the area with lukewarm water by holding the soiled area under a running sink faucet will take care of the problem quickly with little fuss. Save bathing for when your cat's hair coat really needs it.

SUMMARY

By following the suggestions in this chapter, you will provide a safe, fun, healthy environment for your Ragdoll.

CARING FOR YOUR RAGDOLL'S HEALTH

LIFTING YOUR RAGDOLL

All cats have thin skin and fragile ribs and need to be fully supported when lifted up for grooming and loving. Ragdolls are heavy cats and can be injured by incorrect handling. You may have read that Ragdolls will dangle limply if hoisted up under their forelegs. Don't do this to your Ragdoll. The weight of its dangling body pulling against its forelegs and shoulders can cause pain and/or injury. Lifting by the scruff of the neck can cause muscle and skin injury for the same reason. Lifting by grabbing a Ragdoll around the ribs without supporting the hindquarters can injure the rib cage. Lifting under the armpits or by using the forelegs as levers can also cause injury. When picking up your Ragdoll, support the rib cage by placing your hand firmly under it, with one finger between the forelegs pointing toward the chin. At the same time, use your other hand to lift and support the hindquarters. To protect your Ragdoll's welfare, teach your children to lift your Ragdoll only in this manner.

GROOMING

Due to the nature of a true Ragdoll's coat, little grooming is required. However, your Ragdoll will enjoy the personal contact that brushing and combing affords. A weekly grooming

Ragdoll kittens are irresistible. The sweet face of this bicolor lynx is just one reason why Ragdolls are loved so much. Photo by Muncy Smith.

session can be fun for both you and your Ragdoll. We keep grooming supplies in a basket so that they are readily accessible at all times.

Routine grooming includes trimming nails, combing the hair coat, cleaning eyes, ears, and nose, and brushing the teeth. Clip your Ragdoll's nails whenever it is necessary. Use a wide-tooth comb, a slicker brush, and a flea comb to keep your Ragdoll's coat in top condition. Start off with the wide-tooth comb and follow with the flea comb. Use the slicker

Pet shops stock a variety of shampoos that are specially formulated for cats' sensitive systems and that leave a healthy looking coat. Photo courtesy of Four Paws.

brush to fluff up the ruff and tail. Use the cotton swabs and cotton balls to clean eye corners, nose leather, and outer ears. Some people brush their Ragdoll's teeth with special pet toothpaste and brushes. If you regularly groom your Ragdoll, you can easily accustom it to having its teeth brushed. This removes tartar buildup, which can lead to gum disease. Gum disease is not unique to the Ragdoll. It can occur in all breeds of cat. Ask your veterinarian to teach you how to brush, and your Ragdoll will not have to experience being anesthetized and having its teeth cleaned by the veterinarian. Feeding dry food also supposedly helps to prevent and remove tartar buildup.

Finally, it is unusual to need to bathe a Ragdoll, and there is probably no need to do so unless you are planning to enter your Ragdoll in a show. However, some cat owners may wish to give their Ragdolls regular baths. If you want to bathe your Ragdoll, your pet shop can recommend a shampoo specially formulated for cats.

THE BATH

If you bathe your Ragdoll, here are some suggestions. First, increase the heat in the room until it is really toasty. Cats have a higher body temperature than humans and can get chilled easily. If you don't have one, a space heater made especially for the bathroom works very well. While the room is heating, gather pet shampoo, cotton pads, wash cloth, towels, hair dryer, and comb. You will also need a flexible spray shower hose to get the soap off completely. These are available at drug stores.

Although the Ragdoll's coat is not subject to matting as are some other longhaired breeds of cat, occasionally tangles will form here and there. Therefore, before the bath, comb through your Ragdoll's hair coat completely, and remove any tangles by grasping and holding the hair at the base and gently working the hair loose. Never use scissors: even a small nick on a cat's skin can cause big problems because cats have very thin and sensitive skin. Do not skip the pre-comb step, as wet tangles are extremely difficult to remove without damaging the underlying skin. Finally, inspect and clip all claws before the bath.

A great way to accomplish the bath with a minimum of fuss is to put a halter and leash on your Ragdoll the way a professional groomer does and secure the leash to the soap dish in such a way that your Ragdoll can't struggle away from you. But don't secure your Ragdoll near a running faucet. Like any cat, it can be terrified by the rushing water. If you wish, use a small table or box in the tub to raise your Ragdoll to a comfortable working height. Give your Ragdoll a towel or old window screen to stand on so that it won't slip around on the wet sink or tub surface. Any frightened cat that is not being properly managed will try to climb out of a bath by grabbing your chest with its claws, pulling itself over your shoulder and jumping to the floor from your back. To avoid this, always keep one hand on your Ragdoll at all times, and keep it either facing away from you or facing to one side. Don't let it face you. It may try to make a break for it when you least expect it! So, be alert.

Before applying shampoo, you must wet down your cat's hair coat. Cats don't like to be submerged in a sink or tub of water; so don't use this method to wet down the coat. When you begin wetting the hair coat, you will find that it easily repels water, and you must get past this stage before applying the shampoo. Start at the neck and work back

The thick, nonmatting coat makes Ragdolls easy to care for. Just a few strokes with a slicker brush is all it takes to look this well groomed. Photo by Susan Nelson.

toward the tail. While working, talk reassuringly to your Ragdoll. Do not wet the head or face. When wetting down your Ragdoll with a sprayer, keep the spray head close to your Ragdoll's body so that the spray doesn't scare it. If you do not have a sprayer, you will need to pour gallons of warm, not hot, water over and under your Ragdoll to thoroughly wet the coat. A one-quart measuring container can do the trick. Continue to reassure your Ragdoll during this process. A matter-of-fact attitude on your part can be calming. If your Ragdoll begins to shiver, either the room or the water temperature is too cool.

The easiest way to apply shampoo to a wet coat is to dilute it in an empty dish soap bottle before you begin the bath. Dish soap is not appropriate for bathing any cat, so the bottle must be cleaned of any detergent residue. Apply the shampoo, lather up completely, and rinse thoroughly. This step can be repeated if necessary. Unapparent soap residue left after incomplete rinsing can cause itching, with consequent pulling out of the hair coat. Therefore, all soap must be rinsed from the coat by using gallons and gallons of warm water both over and under your Ragdoll, including the underarm and tail areas. During this process, never get water in your cat's ears or eyes. In fact, the only way a cat's face and ears should be washed is with a dampened wash cloth using no shampoo. If you elect to show your Ragdoll, you will learn about "recipes" that others use when doing show grooming. However, the process just described will be more than adequate for any Ragdoll, even show cats.

Pet dental products are available for helping to fight plaque, reduce tartar build-up, and control unpleasant breath. Photo courtesy of Four Paws.

BRUSHING TEETH

Most Ragdolls don't object to having their teeth and gums brushed. Start this early in their lives, and you will save expensive veterinary bills for teeth cleaning, as your veterinarian must use anesthetic before cleaning any cat's teeth. What can be a simple procedure at home can turn into a major one with all the risks attendant to anesthetics if teeth are neglected. Tartar buildup is not unique to Ragdolls; all cats can get tartar buildup on their teeth.

TRIMMING NAILS

A Ragdoll that has its nails trimmed regularly will sit quietly during the process. Make sure that the clipper is sharp enough to make an even cut.

It is a good idea to check all nails once weekly. Often, owners combine this check with a weekly grooming session. The nails on back paws tend to grow slower than the nails on the front paws and usually need to be trimmed less frequently. With experience, you will notice that not every nail will need to be trimmed each week.

To trim nails, you need only grasp your cat's paw and press down on one toe at a time. The claw will pop out for trimming. There are five nails on each front paw and four nails on each back paw. If you look closely, you will see the pink "quick," which is located inside the base of the nail closest to the paw and is shaped like a tiny claw. The next layer

A blue colorpoint whole (unneutered) male named Prince. He weighs almost 15 pounds. Photo by Susan Nelson.

that you will see is a whitened area that seems to surround the quick. Trim only the clear nail that lies beyond both of these areas and that forms the sharp, front part of the claw. If you cut too deeply, you will cause painful bleeding, just as if you cut into the quick of your own nails. A styptic pencil will stop the bleeding, but you will never need to use one if you are always cautious when trimming nails.

SELECTING YOUR VETERINARIAN

Unless you have a veterinarian that you regularly use and trust or that comes highly recommended by someone you respect, the only way to find a good veterinarian is by trial and error. The two keys to an excellent veterinarian are skill and the ability to communicate.

Before bringing their new Ragdoll home, some people go to the extent of interviewing five or six veterinarians before they decide which they prefer. Others simply choose the veterinarian closest to their home. Whatever

you decide, you should feel comfortable talking to your veterinarian. Your veterinarian should welcome your observations and questions. Don't stay with a veterinarian who discounts your observations or questions. You know your Ragdoll and what is and is not unusual behavior. Most veterinarians, even feline specialists, have never seen or treated a Ragdoll. Don't be easily dissuaded from treatment that you believe would benefit your cat.

The connection between you and your veterinarian should feel close if your Ragdoll is receiving

A close-up of Prince. Note the almond-shaped eyes, long whiskers, and large, oval paws. Photo by Susan Nelson.

ongoing treatment of any kind. If you feel estranged from your veterinarian or suspect that your veterinarian does not really care about you and your Ragdoll, talk your feelings over with your veterinarian; if there is no improvement, go elsewhere. Do not continue with a veterinarian who does not handle your Ragdoll gently or require his or her staff to do so. Most towns have at least a few veterinarians. Large cities have scores of veterinarians. Don't settle for impersonal attention. Both you and your Ragdoll deserve kind, professional, knowledgeable care from your veterinarian.

Ragdolls are a unique breed. They are physiologically similar to other pedigreed cats, but they are not the same as non-pedigreed cats that spring from a huge and diverse gene pool. Many Ragdoll breeders believe that Ragdolls are slow to mature. Many also believe that a Ragdoll's immune system is slow to mature. This needs to be taken into consideration when vaccines are given. Never let your veterinarian talk you into a modified live or live vaccine. Also, don't let more than one vaccination be administered at any one visit to your veterinarian. It may take a little longer for you to obtain all necessary vaccinations in this way, but it will be safer for your Ragdoll. Finally, always be certain that the mildest forms of anesthesia are administered when any surgical procedure, such as neutering, is performed.

THE FIRST TRIP TO YOUR VETERINARIAN

Usually, the breeder that you

A large seal lynxpoint male named Ragmeister's Diego. Males may be noticeably larger than females. Photo by Susan Nelson.

bought your Ragdoll from will encourage you to visit the veterinarian as early as possible. This reassures you that you received a healthy kitten and gives your veterinarian a baseline as a measure during future visits.

The first time that you bring your Ragdoll to the veterinarian, you should ask for a complete examination. This may include taking a viral panel to rule out any possibility that a major feline disease is present. All responsible breeders will have no problem with a viral panel, and some would even encourage you to take this action. Write down any questions that you may have before you leave for the veterinarian's office. Don't rely upon your memory, as it is easy to inadvertently move off a topic before all of your questions are completely answered.

At minimum, your veterinarian will take your Ragdoll's temperature, check ears, eyes, nose, listen to the heart and lungs, and examine the teeth and gums and under the tail. Try to bring a fresh fecal sample so that a worm check can be made; however, worming kittens for round worms is usually routine, even if mature adult worms have

A seal lynxpoint enjoying the afternoon sun. Ragdolls should *never* be allowed outside without close supervision. This male is posing in an enclosed backyard. Otherwise, he stays strictly indoors. Photo by Susan Nelson.

not yet migrated to the stomach. Your veterinarian will request your kitten's vaccination record, which the breeder will have supplied to you at the time of purchase. If your breeder has given you instructions regarding spacing of vaccinations and type of vaccine to use, be certain to give a copy to your veterinarian. When you bring in your Ragdoll for any treatment covered by the breeder's instructions, be certain to reiterate those instructions verbally, even though they are already in the veterinarian's file. This avoids any confusion or misunderstandings that could occur and void your Ragdoll's health warranty.

During any trip to the veterinarian, protect your Ragdoll by using its carrier and securing the carrier to the seat with the seat belt. If the seatbelt won't fit all the way around the carrier, tie the seatbelt to the carrier handle. You don't need to put a litter box, food, or water in the carrier with your Ragdoll. Bring these items with you only if the trip is going to take more than an hour or two. Put a toy or two in the carrier, in the event that you must wait for the veterinarian. That way, you can make at least part of the experience of visiting the veterinarian fun for your Ragdoll.

VACCINATIONS

In general, there are four types of vaccinations for cats: the distemper vaccine, the feline leukemia vaccine, the rabies vaccine, and the feline infectious peritonitis vaccine.

Distemper Vaccine

The distemper vaccine is actually three or four vaccines in one. The three-way killed distemper shot vaccinates for panleukopenia (FPV), rhinotracheitis (FVR), and calicivirus (FCV) viruses. All of these viruses are related to upper respiratory disease, which can cause serious illness in any cat. The four-way killed distemper shot includes the previous three vaccines plus *chlamydia*, which is a type of bacteria that causes infection. As we recommended earlier, all vaccines given to Ragdolls should be of the killed variety only. The three-way killed distemper vaccine can be given as early as six weeks of age, and pregnant females can also be vaccinated with three-way killed distemper vaccine. The four-way killed distemper vaccine is usually not given until kittens are at least eight weeks of age. Some breeders believe that it should not be given until twelve weeks of age. When you pick up your kitten, it will probably have had two distemper

Cheers, a ten-week-old seal mitted male, projects every outward appearance of good health. Photo by Alfred Landegger.

shots. Each breeder has his or her own vaccination regimen. Your breeder will tell you when the next distemper shot is due. You must not neglect to have it administered. Normally, a kitten will have three to four distemper shots as a kitten, with an annual booster.

Feline Leukemia Vaccine

There is some controversy regarding the feline leukemia vaccine (FeLV). There have been reports of adverse reactions by Ragdolls to the feline leukemia vaccine. Many breeders are of the mind that since Ragdolls are solely indoor cats and that the feline leukemia virus is caught from contact with other cats, there is little need to risk using this vaccine. Other breeders believe otherwise. Follow the instructions from your breeder, and discuss this question with your veterinarian. If you plan to show your Ragdoll, you will want to consider obtaining this vaccination. Should you decide to vaccinate for the feline leukemia virus, be sure that the virus is of the killed variety only. The leukemia virus vaccine is usually given twice, at one-month intervals at three to five months of age, with a booster annually.

Rabies Vaccine

Some states require that all cats receive the rabies vaccine, in which case you have no choice but to comply. If you live where the rabies vaccine is not required, most breeders believe it is not worth taking the risk, since your Ragdoll will live strictly indoors. Again, discuss this with your breeder and ask your veterinarian. Rabies vaccine is given at four months of age and annually thereafter.

Feline Infectious Peritonitis Vaccine

At this point in time, there is extreme controversy regarding the feline infectious peritonitis (FIP) vaccine. This vaccine is administered by drops placed on the mucous membrane of the nose and, at present, is available only in a modified live form. Some breeders believe that it actually causes FIP and will not allow you to vaccinate your kitten for it. Once again, we believe that since your Ragdoll is going to be indoors only, the need for vaccination is questionable. Follow the instructions of your breeder, as it may affect your health guarantee if you elect to vaccinate for FIP.

ELIMINATING PARASITES

When you bring your Ragdoll home from a responsible breeder,

This seal colorpoint female is wearing an Elizabethan collar, a protective device used to keep animals from biting and scratching themselves or tearing out surgical stitches. Photo by Susan Nelson.

it will be guaranteed free of parasites. Keeping your home and Ragdoll free of parasites will require a lifelong commitment on your part. Maintaining a parasite-free environment is critical to assure your Ragdoll's continuing health and vitality. There are generally three types of parasites that you must either control or eliminate from your home and cat: fleas, worms, and ear mites.

Fleas

Uncontrolled fleas can pose a serious threat to your Ragdoll's well being. This threat can range from annoying itching and scratching with potential loss of hair coat or skin infection, all the way to the potential of flea anemia, whereby your Ragdoll's red blood cells have been depleted to such an extent by fleas feeding on them that your Ragdoll's life could be endangered. This is especially critical with kittens, but adult cats can also be seriously weakened by heavy flea infestation.

Manual Removal of Fleas

Get in the habit of flea combing your Ragdoll regularly. This way, you will spot any flea dirt or fleas before they become a problem. Check your kitten's gums at least once a week. Pale gums indicate possible anemia from flea bites. If you suspect fleas, part the fur on the abdomen and look to see if any fleas run from the light. Don't let this problem get out of hand, as fleas reproduce at a phenomenal rate.

Seal mitted female kitten. A Ragdoll's coloration is not fully mature until the age of around two years. Photo by Muncy Smith.

Parasiticides

As of the publication of this book, new and vastly improved technologies have been developed to deal with flea infestation. Your vet can recommend a product that will greatly aid in keeping your home and your Ragdoll free of fleas.

Carpet Powder and Crystals

An excellent product that we use regularly is boric acid powder or crystals, sprinkled onto all carpets and upholstered surfaces and manually worked into the fibers. If you use it, don't forget to apply it under sofas and chairs and under all sofa and chair cushions as well. It is great for long-term flea control. The boric acid works by drying up the egg and larvae stage of the flea. It does not kill adult fleas. For an effective regimen against fleas, one must also treat the pet.

The flea-fighting product recommended by your vet, along with the boric acid based carpet powder or crystals, will rid your house of fleas and keep your Ragdoll flea free and healthy. Flea powders and sprays that are applied directly to the cat's body can cause tremors and drooling, or worse, and we do not recommend that they be used on your Ragdoll.

WORMS

There are several types of worms that could infest your Ragdoll, robbing it of important nutrients. The two most common are roundworms, which live in the stomach, and tapeworms, which live in the intestines.

Roundworms

When your kitten is three to five weeks old, your breeder will administer the medication necessary to deworm your kitten of roundworms. This medication is given at three and five weeks of age. If your kitten develops an extremely bloated abdomen, roundworms can be suspected. Roundworms are so common that it may take several treatments, spaced regularly within the first year of life, to completely eliminate them. Contact your veterinarian for the proper medication.

Tapeworms

Tapeworms live part of their life cycle in fleas. When your Ragdoll ingests a flea, tape worms can be introduced into its digestive system. Tapeworm segments eventually break off and appear as small white pieces of rice on your kitten's stool, rear hair coat, or anal area. Upon close inspection, you may even see these tapeworm segments moving. Once again, contact your veterinarian for the proper medication.

EAR MITES

When you bring your kitten home, inspect its ears. They should appear clean and free of any brown, dirt-like material. Tiny specks of wax are normal, just as with human ears. However, if you notice any dark brown, waxy clumps developing down inside your kitten's ears, suspect ear mites. Ear mites can be confirmed only by using a microscope. Consult your veterinarian for diagnosis and appropriate medication.

SPAYING AND NEUTERING

All breeders will require you to have a pet-quality kitten spayed or neutered at the appropriate age. Generally, a breeder will withhold registration papers until you have provided proof of spaying or neutering.

There is some discussion in the veterinary community regarding the appropriate age at which to spay or neuter kittens. Most veterinarians continue to suggest that kittens be neutered between four and eight or nine months of age, depending upon gender. Since your Ragdoll will not be outside, there is no reason to neuter before six months of age. Early neutering is done only to help control pet overpopulation and is not an issue with Ragdolls, which are kept only indoors. Follow the recommendations of

A blue colorpoint male relaxing on an enclosed patio. Photo by Susan Nelson.

Products are available for aiding in the elimination of hairballs in cats and kittens. Photo courtesy of Four Paws.

your breeder and veterinarian.

COMMON CAT ILLNESSES
Kitty Colds

The most common problem seen in kittens is sniffling and sneezing. If sniffles and sneezing develop, most veterinarians would recommend that a five- to fifteen-day course of mild antibiotic such as amoxicillin be administered to avoid the possibility of pneumonia. Antibiotics will not stop the course of a cold; they will just prevent complications. The sneezing and sniffling should normally run its course within a week to ten days. Always bring a kitten with a cold to the veterinarian for assessment. Keep your kitten warm and away from drafts if it has, or you suspect that it has, a cold.

Diarrhea

Occasionally, kittens get diarrhea. There are several underlying reasons, ranging from the stress of a new environment to a change in diet. If diarrhea persists for more than 24 hours, consult your veterinarian.

OTHER SYMPTOMS THAT REQUIRE A VET'S ATTENTION

As a survival technique, cats are notorious about not exhibiting signs of illness until they are simply too ill to mask them. So, always take loss of appetite or a listless, depressed demeanor seriously. If your kitten exhibits any of these signs, it is best to see the veterinarian without delay.

Despite the ability to mask symptoms of illness, cats can vomit fairly easily. They vomit for any number of reasons, such as lactose intolerance, ingestion of fur in grooming, spoiled food, or overfeeding. This sort of vomiting usually involves a single episode. Often, you will see fur in the expelled stomach contents. If your healthy kitten suddenly vomits a couple of times and/or exhibits listlessness, see the veterinarian immediately.

SUMMARY

Ragdolls are generally healthy and not prone to illness. Monitor their health just as you would that of any small child who depends upon you for survival. Ragdolls provide us with a wealth of love and devotion, and it is only fair that we return the favor by providing a happy, healthy home environment.

YOUR RAGDOLL'S DIET

There are many ways to approach your Ragdoll's nutritional needs; however, it is up to you to ensure that it has a complete, balanced diet.

When you bring your kitten home, you should follow the advice of your breeder and veterinarian regarding diet. If you decide that you want to alter your Ragdoll's diet, you may opt to use only dry kibbled food or a combination of both dry and canned food. We do not recommend feeding semi-moist foods, and we do not recommend feeding solely canned food. You may decide to forego commercial foods and feed rations that you prepare from scratch. However, realize that rations prepared from scratch have little to nothing in common with the undesirable practice of feeding table scraps, and they may lack some dietary requirements. Many fine pet food companies have researchers who do nothing but work to develop food that provides sound nutrition to kittens and adult cats while retaining palatability.

We cannot emphasize enough that your kitten will have been fed a specific diet by your breeder, and you must adhere to your breeder's instructions when you bring your kitten home. Feed only what the breeder has fed, and adhere to the breeder's feeding schedule, at least until your

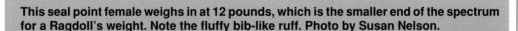

This seal point female weighs in at 12 pounds, which is the smaller end of the spectrum for a Ragdoll's weight. Note the fluffy bib-like ruff. Photo by Susan Nelson.

kitten has become acclimated to its new home.

Cats are carnivores. They need protein and fat to thrive. Do not feed vegetarian foods or dog foods to your Ragdoll, as it must have meat-based foods to attain its proper size and musculature. This is especially critical because Ragdolls typically grow to be quite large, usually at least ten to fifteen pounds for females and fifteen to twenty pounds for males. Breeding Ragdolls are generally slightly smaller. Once a kitten is weaned, it no longer requires milk, and some cats may develop diarrhea from drinking milk. Unlike people, cats cannot thrive on anything except a carnivorous diet.

If you want to change the brand of food that you feed your kitten, go to a large pet supply store and read the labels on lots of different brands of kitten and cat food. With dry food, you will see that the protein content varies between brands, and you should select a food with the highest protein that you can find. Protein should be at least 30 percent, preferably higher. Since your Ragdoll must have lots of quality meat and fat to reach its characteristically large size, we recommend that you feed mostly a high quality, palatable dry food. This type of food is highly concentrated, so more nutrients are delivered per bite compared to a similar quantity of canned food. Canned food labels generally list less than 12 percent protein. Take the time to compare labels, and you will see significant variations in protein, fat, and minerals between brands. Select a food that lists meat products within the first few ingredients. However, no matter what new food you intend to introduce, do so slowly, over about a week or two period, to prevent intestinal upsets and diarrhea.

Food also impacts your kitten's dental health. Dry food tends to mechanically remove tartar from the teeth during feeding, and it is best to offer dry food every day.

Whether to free feed or schedule feeding times is a matter of time and preference. We find that our Ragdolls enjoy a light morning and evening treat of canned food mixed with dry kibble, and we leave dry kibble out for free feeding during the day. Canned food can spoil after sitting out for several hours. While your kitten is growing, keep food readily available, and let it consume as much as it will eat. If you do not want to free feed, you must adhere to a set schedule and always be home at regular meal times. This can present a problem for those working outside the home. When feeding on a schedule, keep the food down for at least 30 minutes so as not to force your Ragdoll to eat quickly and possibly just as quickly regurgitate its meal. Either way you decide to feed, it is up to you to ensure that your Ragdoll consumes adequate, healthy rations.

Finally, have fresh water available at all times. Two bowls in different locations will ensure that water will always be available if one bowl should be accidentally tipped over.

INTRODUCING YOUR NEW RAGDOLL TO YOUR HOME

If at all possible, arrange to pick up your Ragdoll at a time when you can stay at home with it for at least twenty-four hours. Staying home for the first forty-eight hours is even better for your Ragdoll.

THE FIRST DAY

When you arrive at home with your new Ragdoll, there are several things you can do to make it feel comfortable, whether it is a kitten, juvenile, or adult.

First, let your Ragdoll leave its carrier on its own. If it is reticent, encourage it with a toy. If it still doesn't want to come out, sit down in a chair where you can see the carrier and where your Ragdoll can see you, and begin reading a magazine or book. When your kitten comes out of its carrier, relax and talk calmly to it. Praise it. Cuddle and reassure it a bit and, then, place it gently into its new litter box. Scratch the clean litter with your finger a few times to give it an idea of what you expect. This may induce the digging response. If your Ragdoll follows this suggestion, praise it.

Next, show your Ragdoll where you have placed its food and water. After your Ragdoll has visited its litter box and food areas, encourage it back to its litter box area by dragging a tiny toy for it to chase. Do this a few times. That way, you are certain your kitten won't get "lost" when

Chocolate mitted lynx Ragdoll kitten. Photo by Muncy Smith.

it next needs the litter box. At first, have the food within 10 feet of the litter box but no closer than 5 feet. Cats, like us, don't like to eat or drink near where they eliminate.

If your Ragdoll eats when you show it to its food area, you can rest assured that you are well on your way to a happy transition. If your kitten is not interested in food, play with it for a while, cuddle it, and try again later. Lavish praise on your kitten during this time.

The main thing that you want to do during the transition period is to show your Ragdoll that you are trustworthy. The number one sign that your kitten is settling into its new home is its willingness to eat. The next most important sign is its use of the litter box. Keep the litter box within your kitten's view. Your house is a big place to your little

A seal colorpoint and a lilac (frost) bicolor rest after a long day of playing together. Photo by Susan Nelson.

kitten, and if you do not keep the litter box within easy reach, accidents may happen because your Ragdoll will want to stay with you rather than search for its litter box. Its bed should be within 5 to 10 feet of the feeding area, away from the litter box. Keep a few toys out at all times, and play with your Ragdoll in a way that encourages trust.

If you must leave your kitten unattended during the first several weeks, confine it to either your bedroom or any other room that can contain the litter box, food and water, toys, and a bed. The bathroom is a cold room with lots of slick, hard surfaces, and it may not be the safest place to leave your kitten unattended.

THE FIRST NIGHT

There are two ways to handle the first night. You can let the kitten sleep with you, or you can confine it in its room. If you choose the latter, you might expect to hear prolonged crying,

as your kitten only wants to be with you. As long as you have confined it to a safe area, do not be alarmed. Do not respond to your kitten's cries because it needs to learn how to settle itself. If you enter the room frequently to reassure it, you will be training it to continue crying for attention. Eventually, your kitten will fall asleep. When it awakens, it will be anxious to see you. Remember, your kitten has probably never been alone before, and this first night can be difficult for it.

On the other hand, kittens love to sleep with their humans. There are two things to be concerned about when a kitten sleeps with you. First, it will jump down to visit its litter box during the night. You must show it how to get back up on the bed. A stack of books can serve as a "step." Or, you can put a small kitty condo beside the bed. Second, you could roll over and injure your kitten during the night. So, be careful to protect your kitten. Nothing is sweeter than waking up to the bright eyes and tiny purr of a Ragdoll kitten. If you're lucky, maybe you'll even get a tiny kiss on the nose.

THE MULTI-PET ENVIRONMENT

No other cat adjusts as readily to other pets as a Ragdoll. They love cats, dogs, rabbits, and even birds.

When you bring a Ragdoll kitten into a household with existing cats, there will be an adjustment period for the other cats. It is sometimes helpful to keep the new addition in a separate room for a few days. Then, remove it and let the established cats come

time goes by, the other cats will begin to accept your Ragdoll. The Ragdoll's loving, non-aggressive nature makes it a perfect cat to introduce into a multi-cat environment. Existing cats will quickly realize that the new kitten is not a threat. However, to protect your kitten from rough play, keep it separately in its room when you are not present to supervise the interactions. Within two weeks, you should expect to see your Ragdoll playing happily with its house mates. Even so, you should continue to confine your kitten when you are out until you are absolutely certain it has

Seal mitted female. Note the clearly defined, evenly matched front mittens. Photo by Susan Nelson.

in to investigate the scent of the new kitten or cat before actually introducing them to each other. Before the introduction, be sure to clip all front and rear nails to avoid any possible injury during the adjustment period. Your Ragdoll kitten will probably attempt to make friends right away, but the other cats will hiss and rebuff it. Don't be concerned, but do not leave established cats alone with your new addition. As

been accepted or it is at least twelve to sixteen weeks old and more able to escape or fend off aggression.

Dogs will generally be much more accepting of your new Ragdoll. However, dogs can get too rough. So, allow only supervised play until your kitten is at least sixteen weeks old. When bringing a Ragdoll into a home with dogs, rabbits, or birds, the key thing to remember is that

Ragdolls are known for their penchant for snuggling, as this seal mitted Ragdoll named Wally and his young friend demonstrate here. Ragdolls are excellent for children who have been taught how to gently handle cats. Photo by Dodie Strobel.

the Ragdoll does not have the fighting instinct of a regular cat. This leaves it vulnerable to attacks and rough play, which could lead to injury. The safest course is to exercise caution during the introductory period, even following the suggestions outlined above for the multi-cat environment. Many Ragdolls end up regularly napping with the family dog or dogs.

INTRODUCING YOUNG CHILDREN

Young children can also injure Ragdoll kittens by squeezing them too tightly, picking them up incorrectly, or pulling on the head, legs, or tail. When bringing your Ragdoll home, immediately begin to teach your child how to properly handle it. Never let a child pick up a Ragdoll by the neck, leg, or tail. Although a regular kitten or cat may bite or scratch when handled improperly, a Ragdoll may not react at all until it is seriously injured or hurt. It is best to have your child wait until the kitten jumps on its lap for cuddling. Otherwise, the kitten could be injured or frightened by being chased or grasped roughly.

GOING ON VACATION

You will be amazed at how quickly your Ragdoll becomes one of the family. So, you will want to plan carefully for its care when you go on vacation or a business trip. Your Ragdoll cannot care for itself; it depends completely upon you to meet all of its needs.

LEAVING YOUR RAGDOLL AT HOME

If you cannot bring your Ragdoll with you, it will be happiest at home. Never leave a kitten alone for more than twelve hours. An adult Ragdoll can stay alone for a period extending from Saturday morning to Sunday evening, assuming that it readily eats dry food and has at least two bowls of fresh water available at all times. Do not leave out wet food while you are gone because it could spoil and make your cat ill. If you will be gone longer than this, hire a reliable pet sitter. A good friend may also want to take on this responsibility. No matter whether you hire a sitter or use a good friend, a daily visit is essential. Two visits a day is optimum. Be sure to instruct your cat sitter to take some time to comfort and love your Ragdoll, in addition to playing, feeding, watering, and cleaning the litter box. There are trained pet sitters who operate home-based businesses, and you may want to locate one of these individuals. No matter whom you have care for your Ragdoll at home, always leave written instructions and the phone number of your veterinarian in an accessible place.

BOARDING YOUR RAGDOLL

When boarding is the only alternative, try to select a reputable boarding facility that will supply you with several

Purrfectly content...Like many other cats, your Ragdoll may prefer your bed to its own. Photo by Alfred Landegger.

references. Then, check out the references. Don't trust your Ragdoll to a boarding facility that you have not checked out thoroughly. Beware of facilities that cut corners on comfort, feeding, and sanitation. If a facility will not let you inspect the entire kennel, don't leave your Ragdoll.

One of the main dangers of boarding is the transmission of disease between animals. If the facility does not insist that all cats have health certificates with up-to-date vaccinations, don't risk your Ragdoll's health. Also, a well-run kennel, like a well-run veterinary hospital, should not have a heavy litter box odor. The cleanest kennels will have little or no odor. Ideally, you should select a boarding facility well in advance of the time that you will need to board your Ragdoll, and inspect it one more time shortly before your trip.

TAKING YOUR RAGDOLL ALONG

Many Ragdolls have been trained to be wonderful travelers, whether by motor home, automobile, or airline. If traveling with your Ragdoll is in your future plans, accustom it early on to public life. Purchase a halter and leash and gradually let your Ragdoll become accustomed to wearing them. Give it a treat when it maintains a relaxed attitude.

Take it for rides in the car and bring it to visit neighbors and friends. This helps train your Ragdoll to be comfortable in unfamiliar situations. The more exposure you give your Ragdoll, the more relaxed and enjoyable it will be as a travel companion.

Just one note of caution: Don't leave your Ragdoll alone in a car, as it can be overcome by heat prostration quicker than you would believe possible. This holds true for other pets as well.

A Ragdoll quartet: seal mitted, blue mitted lynxs, and seal colorpoint lynx. Photo by Susan Nelson.

Be certain to bring a supply of your Ragdoll's regular litter, food, and water to prevent bouts of diarrhea while traveling. Pack its favorite toys and blanket or bed. Bring its grooming tools. Make arrangements to stay at accommodations that welcome pets. As soon as you check into your room, hang out the "do not disturb sign" to minimize the chance that a service person may inadvertently let your Ragdoll out while you are at dinner or the pool. Do not leave your Ragdoll alone in unfamiliar surroundings for an extended period of time. Be aware that your Ragdoll may have trouble adjusting its sleep schedule if you vacation in another time zone. Follow all of these suggestions, and you will thoroughly enjoy taking your Ragdoll along on vacation.

Above: Blue mitted male kitten playfully swiping at a toy. Offer your Ragdoll a variety of toys to keep it occupied. Photo by Susan Nielsen. *Below:* A rare tortie lynxpoint Ragdoll kitten. Photo by Muncy Smith.

THINGS TO CONSIDER ABOUT BREEDING RAGDOLLS

Breeding Ragdolls is not something to enter into lightly. Although the thought of cuddly kittens playing in your living room sounds tempting, there is a lot more involved in breeding than meets the eye. What follows is a quick breeding overview. After reading the overview, we suggest that you think long and hard before you make any decision to breed Ragdolls. If you do decide to breed Ragdolls, contact the Ragdoll Fanciers Club International (RFCI) for more information and insight into breeding challenges.

Before you decide whether to breed, do lots of homework first. After all, you are going to gamble a considerable amount of money to establish a breeding pair in your home, including all the equipment that you will need, such as a stud cage, queening cage, scales, special diet, license,

cattery registration, and so forth. Therefore, contact a wide range of breeders, and don't be afraid to ask questions. Do not buy from the first breeder that you interview. Talk with veterinarians and discuss the costs associated with breeding complications. Read all the books that you can on breeding purebred cats and feline husbandry in general.

Take your time. Not all breeders will be able to produce the top-quality breeding pair that you must have to establish a reputable cattery. Examine the entire pedigree of each breeding Ragdoll you are considering, and if you do not know enough about the particular Ragdolls listed on the pedigree, ask for the names and addresses of the registered owners, and phone them to discuss their bloodlines. And remember, the relationship that you establish as a new breeder

Breeding purebred cats requires a considerable investment in both money and time. It is essential that you carefully weigh all of the factors involved before you make any decisions about starting a breeding program. Photo by Susan Nelson.

with your selling breeder will be ongoing. You need to feel absolutely comfortable calling your breeder any time of the day or night, if necessary. So, the breeder that you eventually buy from must be someone that you trust to provide you with quality breeding stock and with whom you can communicate easily, without reservation. Anything less will jeopardize your successful entry into breeding.

BREEDING COSTS

When purchasing breeding Ragdolls, you can expect to pay two to three times the amount that you would for a pet-quality Ragdoll. Some breeders believe that whatever your yearly veterinarian's bill would be for one Ragdoll, triple it for a breeding pair. Barring any unforeseen events, such as a retained placenta or difficult birth, both of which require veterinary assistance, the cost of deworming and vaccinating your kittens as well as caring for the general health care of your breeders can be a major expense. When breeding cats, you must feed premium food and supplemental vitamins, which is another cost that must be considered. A preventive flea control program must be maintained and adequate stocks of litter and nursing and weaning supplies must be kept on hand at all times. Failure to provide your breeding cats and kittens with these minimal requirements will negatively impact the reputation of your cattery and you as a breeder. To enhance your cattery reputation, you also must regularly enter your breeding cats and best kittens into cat shows.

Champion Miss Ashley of Ragmeister, a seal mitted female, with Chloe, her six-week-old daughter. Photo by Susan Nelson.

Entry fees, per show, for two cats or kittens and grooming space can add up to a pretty penny, not counting transportation, food, show supplies, and, possibly, motel expenses.

THE BREEDING PAIR

Some Ragdoll associations require you to purchase a breeding pair of Ragdolls before you may ethically breed at all. This can present a real problem to the novice, as breeding males (often referred to as studs or whole males) must be kept isolated to prevent urine spraying in the house, and the spray of a whole male is particularly offensive. Although not all whole males spray, you must have an alternative living quarters for your male should he do so. This behavior may not occur until your male is eight months old or older and becomes sexually active. However, most whole males spend their entire lives in stud cages. Without three or four females to keep company with a breeding male, a solo male in a stud cage leads a bleak existence. Some small breeders solve this problem by introducing a spayed or neutered companion cat into the stud cage. If you plan to do this, it is best to have them grow up together as kittens. In any event, you must enter the stud cage at least once daily to tend to the emotional needs of your stud male.

Whole females (often referred to as queens) can also spray, although their spray is not as pungent. Spraying is a natural behavior of breeding animals, as they use this scent to attract a mate. Whole females will often "call" when they are in heat. This can involve loud yowling and crying all through the night, which is an important consideration for you, your family, and your close neighbors. Regarding such noise, be aware that each time a breeding or rebreeding occurs, the female screams loudly. Your

A female seal colorpoint. Ragdolls that are selected for a breeding program must be as genetically diverse as possible. Photo by Gary Strobel.

A blue bicolor queen nursing her kittens. In their first weeks of life, kittens receive all of their essential nutrients from their mother's milk. Photo by Muncy Smith.

family and neighbors may not appreciate this screaming, especially during the early morning hours. Like stud males, whole females require love and attention from you on a daily basis.

If your city or town has special ordinances governing the breeding of animals, unhappy neighbors could attempt to shut down your breeding program, resulting in the loss of your entire investment.

SPACE REQUIREMENTS

As if yowling, spraying cats are not daunting enough, there are critical space requirements when it comes to breeding Ragdolls. As discussed above, you must be able to provide a separate living area for the breeding male, should he be a sprayer. You must also provide a "queening" area in a warm, quiet location of your home for the birth and nursing of the kittens. Finally, you must be able to accommodate toddling kittens in a totally safe space. Proper breeding practices require that queens and their litters be separated from other litters until the weaning stage has passed. If you keep three or four breeding females, this means that you may have to separately accommodate and clean up after as many as four litters at any one time.

TIME REQUIREMENTS

The time required for proper cattery maintenance and breeding saps nearly all free time available and ties you completely to your favorite litter scoop, bleach bucket, and mop. Additionally, if you work away from the home, you may have a difficult time arranging to be present for each birth, but you must be present to provide whatever assistance your queen needs. When each litter is born, there is the possibility that supplemental feedings will be required; and, on occasion, if the queen is not able to nurse her kittens, you must take over the duties of the mother. This involves feeding the kittens every two to four hours around the clock as well as stimulating the kittens to urinate and defecate after each feeding. These complications are unlikely to occur; but, nonetheless, they are possible and must be taken into consideration

Four-week-old seal mitted kittens. Note the fluffy quality of their fur. Photo by Muncy Smith.

Bright-eyed and bushy tailed, a "lotta lynxs" pose for the camera. Photo by Susan Nelson.

A blue lynx bicolor female. The term "lynx" simply refers to the striped pattern, as is evident on this Ragdoll's forehead. Photo by Susan Nelson.

when deciding whether to breed cats. Even if supplemental feedings are not required, kittens must be weighed and examined at least twice each day. Even with this level of care, you can lose a kitten quickly if it becomes chilled, and you may not realize that a kitten is in trouble until it is too late.

When the kittens are being weaned, you must devote additional time to assure that each kitten is adjusting appropriately to its new diet, eating well, and continuing to gain weight. Some kittens refuse to start eating solid foods and if not monitored carefully and fed by

hand, they can whither and die before you realize that there is a problem.

Although Ragdolls are inherently sweet and loving, a good portion of their personality development will depend on you spending hours and hours of time socializing them through cuddling and play. Because breeding is so time intensive and your presence is nearly always needed, you will seldom be able to leave the house for longer than it takes to have dinner with friends. All of this omits the twice-daily feeding, water changing, litter box chores, and the additional time that you will need to spend vacuuming,

Vivian, a seal bicolor female. As is true for any other cat breed, Ragdolls selected for breeding must be in perfect health and top condition. Photo by Susan Nelson.

cleaning, and disinfecting your home and the breeding quarters, to ward off disease. All this having been said, breeding Ragdolls can be enormously satisfying.

GENETIC CONSIDERATIONS

If you should decide to breed Ragdolls, it is important that the genetic makeup of your male and female be as diverse as possible. As with any other breed of cat, using animals that are closely related for breeding can cause genetic health problems. Due to the fact that the Ragdoll breed is only about 30 years old, it is especially important not to breed from close genetic lines. If you are unable to obtain a quality, unrelated but genetically compatible breeding pair from one breeder, that breeder can arrange for another to supply the missing cat.

SUMMARY

You may feel that we have presented an unnecessarily bleak picture of what breeding entails, but we assure you that all of the above topics must be carefully considered before you decide to enter into any breeding program. Lots of people have entered the breeding field and left after only a few months or years when they realized all that it entailed. We want you to know the obligations involved before you invest your time and money into breeding.

SHOWING YOUR RAGDOLL

WHY SHOW YOUR RAGDOLL?

Assuming that you purchase a show-quality Ragdoll, showing your Ragdoll can be some of the most fun you've ever experienced. This is because you will meet some incredibly nice people and have a chance to show off your Ragdoll to others. You will advance the Ragdoll breed by exposing others to this relatively new breed of cat. At the same time, you will have a chance to meet people from all over the country and make new friends in the process. Your Ragdoll may even win a couple of ribbons!

WHAT DO I NEED TO DO FIRST?

The first step on the way to showing your Ragdoll is to obtain what your breeder would call a show-quality Ragdoll. Your breeder should be able to discern whether or not your Ragdoll possesses the necessary show qualities. Depending upon the breeder, you will either need to pay a premium over the standard pet-quality price or agree to advertise the cattery during each show that you attend. This would usually entail putting some of the breeder's business cards on your show cage and making a point of

Co-author Susan Nelson confers with a show judge after receiving a "final" on her seal mitted female named Ragmeister's Dolly. Photo by Kathy Lam.

You will often find your Ragdoll resting in unusual places when your lap is not available, as this seal colorpoint shows us. Photo by Carla Applegate.

telling those who stop to talk with you where you obtained your Ragdoll. When you purchase a show-quality Ragdoll, your breeder will supply the necessary registration paperwork immediately. You will still need to spay or neuter your Ragdoll at the appropriate age, in accord with the purchase contract. Nearly all cat associations require your kitten to be at least four months of age, in good health, tested and free from feline leukemia, and inoculated against specific diseases before you can show it.

HOW DO I FIND OUT ABOUT SHOWS?

There are several different cat associations that sponsor cat shows. You will need to register your kitten in each association in which you intend to show. So, while your kitten is growing, you may want to contact the various associations and inquire about upcoming shows that are being

sponsored in your area. You can also look in *Cat Fancy* or *Cats Magazine* to find out about show dates. Decide which shows you want to enter, and mark your calendar. Showing can become very expensive, even if you attend only one show each month, but some shows offer a discounted entry fee if you enter before a specific date. There is transportation expense, and you must eat during the eight to twelve hours that you will be at the show. Many shows will be a good distance from your home. If you need to stay overnight, there will be additional motel and restaurant expenses to consider. For all of these reasons, it is a good idea to find out about upcoming show dates as early as possible.

REGISTERING YOUR RAGDOLL FOR THE SHOW

If the association sponsoring

Seal mitted female. The Ragdoll's large blue eyes are moderately wide set. Photo by Susan Nelson.

the show that you want to enter is different from the one in which your Ragdoll is registered, you must register your cat in the new association. This is a one-time requirement and involves sending a copy of your original registration papers, with a three-generation pedigree, to the new association along with the registration fee. You will receive your new registration papers in the mail, generally within a week or two. Keep them in a safe place along with your Ragdoll's other important papers.

SHOW SUPPLIES
Cage Curtains

When you arrive at the show, you must check in, obtain a show program, and locate the benching cage that has been assigned to your Ragdoll. You will have brought with you the required "cage curtains." At minimum, these curtains must cover the outside and top of your cage, and you need a show blanket or towel for the bottom of your cage. Most experienced show people use only show curtains that also cover the inside of the cage, to protect their cats from cold show halls and any germs that might be on the benching cage wire. You can find the dimensions of the cages on the show's flyer. These are usually standard, so once you have a set of cage curtains, you can use them repeatedly. You can make your own curtains, or you can

The requirements for championship titles vary from one association to another. It is up to you to familiarize yourself with the points required for your Ragdoll to reach each championship level. Photo by Susan Nelson.

A Ragdoll photographed during a supervised outing in the garden. Photo by Marie Palm.

and can be purchased at pet stores. You will also need small food and water dishes for inside the cage. Take along your cat's favorite food as well as a bottle of the water it usually drinks. You may also want to put in a soft, plush bed or pillow for your cat to sleep on or hide behind. These are available from show vendors, and you can select one that matches your cage curtains if you don't have one when you attend your first show. We have seen exhibitors use a doll bed inside the benching cage, and cats seem to love them. Bring along a couple of your Ragdoll's favorite small toys so that it has something to play with in the cage. There are hammocks and hanging carpeted ledges that you can purchase or make for your cage, and you will see these in some exhibitors' cages when you visit your first cat show. Some cats prefer to lounge on these while waiting to be called to each show ring. Let your fantasy run wild when decorating your Ragdoll's show cage, and you will have even more fun at each show!

Grooming Supplies
Bring your usual grooming aids to the show in your show tote. These will include a wire slicker brush, metal comb, and flea comb. The flea comb's fine teeth are good for completely separating your Ragdoll's fur coat before using the slicker brush to fluff ruff and tail before each show ring. You will also need cotton swabs and/or cotton balls or cotton squares for any last minute

buy a set at most shows, but you must obtain them before your first show. Don't plan to buy them at your first show. Since it is a good idea to observe at least one show before you begin showing, you can use that opportunity to purchase show curtains from a show vendor or get ideas for making your own set.

Cage Supplies
There are a few things that you must have for inside your Ragdoll's show cage and a few things that are optional. You will need to take along a small litter box and the litter your kitten prefers for inside the cage. Small litter boxes are about 12" x 15"

cleaning of the ears, nose, or eyes. You will pick up tips from other show people as you become more accustomed to showing. There are lots of powders, sprays, and grooming tricks that you will learn about as you gain more experience.

Disinfectant

Never go to a show without a spray bottle of disinfectant and a roll of paper towels. People may want to pet and touch your Ragdoll, and you have every right to refuse. However, if you would like them to be able to experience a Ragdoll up close, it is of the utmost importance that at least their hands be disinfected before coming in contact with your Ragdoll. You have no idea how many other cats they may have touched, and upper respiratory infections are spread easily at shows. You will see the importance of this measure at every judge's table, as they spray their own hands and clothes as well as the judging platform in between each cat that they handle. You should use the disinfectant frequently at the show as well. It can be purchased in a concentrated form from your veterinarian, who stocks it to use on all hard surfaces before examining the next patient. Simply tell the vet that you want to purchase some disinfectant to use for disease protection while showing your Ragdoll.

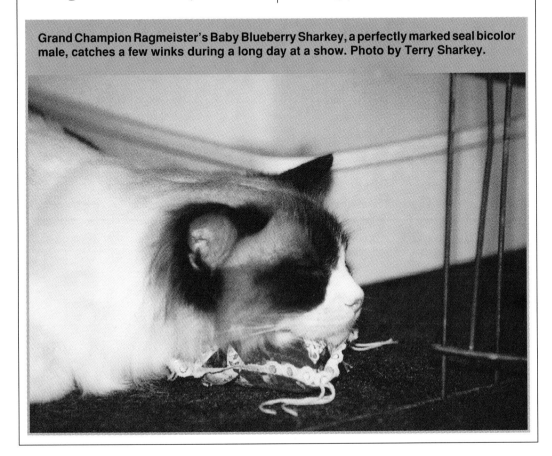

Grand Champion Ragmeister's Baby Blueberry Sharkey, a perfectly marked seal bicolor male, catches a few winks during a long day at a show. Photo by Terry Sharkey.

SHOW GROOMING
The Bath

The show bath is required by all associations because your Ragdoll must be absolutely clean and free of any parasites. You can do a simple show bath with a hypoallergenic shampoo or you can do an elaborate show bath with many different steps. The choice is yours. You may want to give a shorter bath the first few

We have already given a detailed explanation of how to bathe your Ragdoll. You will learn more about the show bath as you continue showing and talking with others. You may want to have someone help you give the bath and assist with the drying process. Drying can be accomplished either by placing your Ragdoll in its carrier and blowing in warm air with a hair dryer, or you can hold your

These two four-week-old blue mitted lynxs are the embodiment of a Ragdoll kitten's personality and charm. Photo by Susan Nelson.

times you show so that your Ragdoll becomes accustomed to the process slowly. You will be able to decide what approach you want to take once you have spoken with other show exhibitors and observed your Ragdoll's reaction to being bathed.

Ragdoll on your lap in a dry towel and gradually blow it dry, using a wide-tooth comb to gently separate hair clumps and making certain that your hand is always between the blow dryer and your Ragdoll, to assure that you don't overheat or burn your cat.

Clipping the Nails

All associations require that each nail be clipped before any cat can be shown. We have discussed nail clipping previously. Do not clip into the quick, but make certain that you thoroughly trim the clear area that forms the front of the claw. Your cat may be nervous at the cat show, and it is important that its nails be a length that cannot hurt you or the judges.

that you may observe inside your cat's ears. Do not go any lower than you can see. Some people purchase a special solution at the pet store to use for this purpose.

Cleaning the Mouth

If you plan to show your cat, you should begin a program of brushing its teeth while it is still a kitten. That way, you will never need to scrape tartar from your cat's teeth when preparing for a

Priscilla, a seal colorpoint female. Ragdolls are gentle cats with laid-back personalities. Photo by Susan Nelson.

Cleaning the Ears

Ears must be clean and free of parasites such as ear mites. We have discussed ear mites previously, and it is unlikely that your Ragdoll will ever contract them. A certain amount of waxy build-up is normal, and using a cotton swab, you can gently remove any tiny clumps of wax

show. Simply use a special pet toothbrush and pet toothpaste, and brush as usual. Do not use human toothpaste on your cat's teeth.

AT THE SHOW
What To Do When You Arrive

When you arrive, you will proceed to the registration table

and pick up your "show packet." This packet will include an entry number, which your Ragdoll will be known by throughout the day. Proceed to the "benching area," which is the set of cages where your Ragdoll will be housed for the day, and locate the cage with that number. Immediately write the entry number on your hand, as you will need to refer to it countless times during the day. Begin to set up your cage by putting down your Ragdoll's show blanket or towel, hanging your curtains, and putting out the cage supplies. Place your Ragdoll's number on the front of its cage. Then, place your Ragdoll into its cage, verbally assuring it that everything is fine, petting it in a matter-of-fact way, and letting it

A seal mitted female named Amber. Ragdolls belong indoors. No matter how small or large your living quarters, your Ragdoll will be happiest and safest at home indoors. Photo by Gary Strobel.

This Ragdoll is feeling frisky. Note the huge, fluffy tail typical of Ragdolls. Photo by Susan Nelson.

Lilac (frost) bicolor female. Photo by Kathy Lam.

get accustomed to its new surroundings.

Next, locate your Ragdoll's entry information listed inside the show program, and make certain that each item of information is correct. If it is not, you must speak with the clerk of each ring and request that the information be corrected. Otherwise, you may not be able to claim any winners' ribbons that your Ragdoll may receive during that show. Then, take a few minutes to go over the show schedule listed on the program and determine approximately when your Ragdoll will be called to each ring. No times are listed on the program, and the judging progression depends entirely on when each judge begins and how quickly the judging of each class proceeds. We have found that the best way to keep track of when your Ragdoll must be present at each ring for judging is to circle your Ragdoll's entry class on each judge's schedule; otherwise, the hustle and bustle of the show hall could result in your missing a judging call.

Be aware that unless you paid extra for grooming space, you will need to do most of your grooming in your lap. Bring a towel for this purpose or invest in a portable grooming table. There will be no space for you to spread your things out. The benching aisles are fairly narrow, and you will need to put all of your supplies, carrier, and show tote under the benching table.

The Show Rings

A typical show consists of approximately six rings. Each of these rings is an entire cat show unto itself. There is one judge in each ring, and by the end of the day, that judge will have evaluated all the cats in the show hall. As the day progresses, your Ragdoll's number will be called out over the loudspeaker along with instructions such as, "Cats 19 through 28, this is your first call for ring 3." Quickly back brush and fluff up your Ragdoll and, in a timely manner, carry it to the ring to which it has been called. There will be a cage at that ring with your number on top of it. Place your Ragdoll in the cage and have a seat in the audience section. Try to sit in the front row, in view of your Ragdoll. It will be able to see you, and knowing you are present will provide some comfort if your Ragdoll is a bit nervous. It is also a good idea to sit in the front row because you can hear exactly what the judge is saying. If you listen closely, you will learn a great deal. It is improper to speak to a judge throughout this process, unless you are spoken to first.

A CFA (Cat Fanciers' Association) judge examining a seal bicolor Ragdoll. Cat shows are informative and fun. They can provide the opportunity for you to share your interest in Ragdolls with other Ragdoll fanciers. Photo by Susan Nelson.

Each cat association has its own requirements for champion, grand champion, supreme grand champion, etc. Even the championship titles vary from association to association. It is up to you to become familiar with the points required for your Ragdoll to reach each championship level. Naturally, you must keep track of your Ragdoll's points if you want to claim any of its titles.

When the judging is finished, there will be an announcement that your cat may be returned to its cage. At this time, you must remove the cat without speaking to the judge, and take it back to your benching area. If your cat is lucky enough to "final" in a ring, your number will be called again at some point during the day to return to that ring. Sometimes, the specific numbers are not called. There is simply a general announcement that "Finals are posted in ring 1, please check your numbers." Be certain to walk to that ring and actually check for your Ragdoll's number, as signs and decorations sometimes will block your view.

It is important that you listen to the announcements all day long and walk to the various rings to check on judging progress. You can check on judging progress by looking at the entry numbers of the cats caged in that particular judging ring, looking up some of the numbers in the show catalog, and deciding what class is being judged at that time.

What the Judges Will Look for in Your Ragdoll

Before the judge even takes your Ragdoll out of its cage, he or she will have made some assessments as far as bone and coat appearance are concerned. When the judge removes your Ragdoll from its cage, he or she will be noticing temperament and weight. Once the judge places your Ragdoll on the judging platform, he or she will carefully check the head for proper conformation and ears for proper placement. To do this, the judge will often use a toy to attract the cat's attention, moving the toy so that the cat's head can be examined from all angles. Eye color is also checked at this time. The coat and overall feel of the body is checked by running the hands over the Ragdoll's body. At this point, the judge may pick the cat up and hold it aloft to examine its face more closely before returning it to its cage. You will see the judge and the judge's assistant making notes about

your Ragdoll. At some point, the assistant will announce that your Ragdoll can "go back."

Cleaning Up and Leaving the Show Hall

Be considerate of the sponsoring cat club and clean up your area before you leave. There are trash cans provided strategically throughout the show hall for this purpose, and cleaning up will be easier if you attend to this task throughout the day. This is particularly important because if the show hall is left in clean condition, the owners will be more likely to rent it out again when that cat club wishes to sponsor another association show. Be sure to get the phone numbers or business cards of people whom you've met at the show, as you may want to keep in touch and discuss upcoming shows and showing techniques with them.

ENJOY YOUR SHOWING EXPERIENCE

We hope that you will enjoy your showing experience. It is hard work preparing for a show, getting up early in the morning, and driving to a show, but we wish that we had the time to enter more cat shows. We have found that the best way to approach showing is simply to prepare thoroughly for each show, get set up quickly when you arrive, and, then, relax and enjoy the camaraderie of being with a show hall full of beautiful cats and bona fide cat lovers!

ABOUT THE AUTHORS

Gary Strobel is a school teacher in Southern California. As a hobby, Gary has been involved with animals and animal husbandry since he was a young boy. Gary started Ragmeister Ragdolls in 1991 with his first female Ragdoll named Lucy, a lilac bi-color. Located in beautiful San Diego, California, Ragmeister Ragdolls has become an internationally recognized and respected breeder of the Ragdoll cat. Gary is dedicated to improving the Ragdoll breed and believes that the special "Ragdoll personality" is the top breeding priority. Gary's love of the Ragdoll breed and his enthusiasm in educating the public in regard to the uniqueness of the Ragdoll was his inspiration for writing this book.

Susan Nelson is an attorney and award-winning wildlife photographer who has owned and loved cats for nearly five decades. She was planning to add either a

Co-author Susan Nelson with Chloe, her six-week-old seal colorpoint female. Photo by Kathy Lam.

Co-author Gary Strobel, center, pictured at a cat show with fellow Ragdoll fanciers Roy and Muncy Smith. The Ragdolls are Ragmeister's Hawkeye, a blue mitted lynx male, and Ragmeister's BJ Honeycutt, a lilac bicolor male. Photo by Susan Nelson.

Himalayan or Maine Coon kitten to her home when an article in *Cat Fancy* magazine about the Ragdoll breed aroused her curiosity. After learning that there were no published books about Ragdoll cats, Susan began searching for information about them. Her search led to Ragmeister Ragdolls of Southern California. There, she met Gary Strobel and discovered that Ragdolls truly do possess unique temperament, size, and beauty. Since that time, she and her husband have acquired three Ragdolls. Susan spends a large portion of her free time showing her Ragdolls and co-authored this book to share her love of Ragdolls.

INDEX